TRADESMAN'S EXIT

TRADESMAN'S EXIT

MICHAEL BARTHOLOMEW-BIGGS

Shoestring  Press

Typeset and printed by Q3 Print Project Management Ltd,
Loughborough, Leics
(01509) 213456

Published by Shoestring Press
19 Devonshire Avenue, Beeston, Nottingham, NG9 1BS
(0115) 925 1827
www.shoestringpress.co.uk

To Nancy
with love and thanks yet again

CONTENTS

AT THE BUTCHER'S PALACE OF VARIETIES

I was never troubled
as a toddler by the drips
from rabbits with small bloody noses
waiting for a turn
to have their skins pulled inside out
like my raincoat in the cloakroom.

I learned to take for granted
contact with both flesh and money
was taboo and caged cashiers
must have each price recited
with panache to match the twirled
moustaches of a ringmaster.

When sawdust disappeared
and rabbits on trapezes vanished
with money-changers in straw hats
then Pantaloon went too
leaving simply sausages
and Grand-Guignol declined to sideshow.

I watch as Mr Hudson
prepares a pair of Barnsley chops;
he's like a surgeon in Crimea
with his busy bonesaw.
Meticulous, he trims the fat
as if he's read Leviticus.

Oddly, it's his turn
to show a trace of nasal bleeding
above a nice plump lip. He mutters
what I owe, stiff-mouthed,
a second-string ventriloquist
with nowhere now to throw his voice.

AHEAD ON POINTS

A face that caught a thousand clips
from heavy gloves on better boxers
over fifty years ago
looked up beside the hot-cross buns.
Meanwhile the stubby body, stooping
in the queue ahead of me
stayed crouching low a moment longer
gathering an extra basket
to jab left-handed at my solar plexus.

I parried with a thankyou but
his kindness, slipped in underneath
my guard, had knocked my gratitude
off-balance, giving it the grace and style
of a schoolgirl's round-arm slap.
A toothless grin spread out below
his shape-free nose, and pouchy cheeks
unwrinkled with the guileless pleasure
of a baby playing pat-a-cake.

SAY IT WITH ....

What you done wrong then, mate?
There's perfect rhythm
in this perfect stranger's query
as he sees me on the Essex Road,
one arm full of orange Alstromeria.

Well, let's just say I hope it works.
I accept his premise, dodging detail
and colluding with his blunt assumption
that marriage is guerrilla war
of floral versus verbal weapons.

I could stretch loose prejudice,
extend his list of peccadillos:
She heard I'd grumbled at her cooking
while I showered with her sister ...
Or *I missed my boyfriend's birthday ...*

Cheap-shoe streets of shabby pubs
are grimed by quiet pessimism:
wry humour is an easy solvent,
wiping off the surface worst, at best.
Under pavements and all nearby floorboards
things are scuttling
where you wouldn't want to put your hand.

In the butcher's, Mr Hudson beams.
He's sharp as his best boning-knife –
and about as unsurprising:
You didn't need to bring me flowers.

REDUCED

"If you come around, I said to him
last night, *you'll have to take me as I am
'cos I look a right state."* She half-laughed
but her chin clenched in defiance at the recall
of bracing for a not-so-playful jab.

Now, sitting at the supermarket check-out,
she was in control of half the story.

Did he arrive? And take her as she had been
hoping that he would? Or did the bruising
on the surface of the merchandise
provoke a jibe about its sell-by date?

The till she used was not set up to total
her own good points: she always half-expected
somebody to say she had short-changed them.

AT THE SUPERMARKET

Suddenly
you're with me by the vegetables
wondering what yams are like.

A string of garlic tugs
my memory and you
are pointing out red onions,
the sort they sold to us
on the Côte Emeraude
where still windmills stand
in line beside the sea
with hands across their faces.

Something French –
or, even better, Spanish –
could always stir your appetite:

olives pressed out bead by bead
as tilted screw-thread trunks are tightened
each time the sun comes round again
to shimmer over silver groves
amid vibrations of red dust;
or springtime vines, like little trees
painted with a pruning knife,
tensed as upraised wiry arms
for squeezing yet another season's
essence from dry ground to pour
again from autumn-opened hands.

I sense your smile
of pleasure as we notice
the plum tomatoes have arrived.

WALNUTS

I chose not to believe you
when you told me there were walnuts
growing on those trees beside the road.
Yet I possessed no better explanation
than a confidently vague pronouncement
they must flourish only further south.
So then we had to put it to the test:
crack and prise the kernel from its cavity,
hands brown-stained with juices,
proving you'd been right.
My apology was grudging.

The blue lights proved it too.
Until the ambulance arrived
I'd been unwilling to accept that you
had recognized again ahead of me
what kind of fruit was ripening to fall
when you complained about the ache that clenched
and swelled inside the hollow of your chest.
In A&E I hovered while they set about
persuading you with bruises
to say you'd got it wrong,
my apology irrelevant.

CHAOS

From far enough above no one can see
the jagged edges; fractals halve and fold
a finite coastline infinitely.
Boundary layers round events confine
each small disturbance hidden by streamlines
in incompressible and shock-free time.

It's been x months – that's all the neighbours know:
do they suppose that grass has grown on sorrow
like a seamless robe and made a sad slope
smooth enough to climb to get from then to now?
In fact, he's slid and scrambled daily for a purchase,
ignoring grit that's grazed his two hands' palms,
on the foreign cliff-face of her absence.

HIGH WIRE

Their show is on the road.
His job is the rigging; every day
he sets out the stall, the props.
Takes care of the tension.
On the hour she climbs the ladder
slides her toe out on the line
while he saunters through the audience.

She's still learning; always
he's expecting more. She surely knows
by now the way to take a fall?
And yes she's getting better,
doing simple tricks on calm days:
on gusty ones the basic act
is balancing adrenaline and bile.

Today he's left the wire too slack
again; halfway across it sags and sways
as if she is a fish he's playing.
But still she needs to see him,
preferably smiling,
or terrors rush Niagara-like beneath her,
the drag of her anxiety stretching
final steplengths bowstring steep
between her and the end of the performance.

N by NW in N1
An Alfred Hitchcock memorial at the old Gainsborough Studios

I met a resident of Islington
who said: *A vast and rusting head of steel*
looms in a courtyard; trunkless on a plinth,
where Gainsborough Studios once stood, its round
unwrinkled scalp and cheeks and baby pout
show that the welder knew those features well
which still survive in countless TV reruns,
mocking the fears of which he knew too much.

The birds and blank rear windows might look down
on Hoxton's Ozymandias; film buffs
look up to him – would still revere his craft
if none but this remained: a distant biplane
that's spraying crops and Cary Grant, alone
with white and waving wheat stretched far away.

GUNPLAY
At the Old Operating Theatre Museum, St Thomas's Hospital

Being shot on film
used to spin them round
like Tom or Jerry or the chamber
on the Colt the hero played with,
cleanly dead before they hit the dirt.
Now screen victims spray like tomcats
demonstrating murder makes a mess.

In fact, you'd be amazed
what damage human tissue
does to bullets. Bones deflect
a missile deeper into muscle
nearly at the speed of sound; but nerves
react like lightning: screams wound up
by entry wounds can snap before an exit.

A hospital museum
exhibits leaden messes
picked from limbs by Crimea surgeons,
then driven into surplus corpses
for extra practice at extracting shrapnel.
The art of treating gunshot wounds
has much advanced this century in Europe.

The operating table
holds targets up to marksmen
licensed to eliminate
all threats that won't go quietly:
a scrabble in this metaphoric barrel
might scrape some parable endorsing
a taste for pulling triggers now and then.

221b

Mysteries swirl underneath the door.
Anxious clients clatter up the stair.
Hawklike Holmes is striding round the floor
while faithful Watson's busy being there.

Baker Street is blanketed in fog.
Mysteries swirl underneath the door.
Troubled by the conduct of a dog
hawklike Holmes is striding round the floor.

Smoke three pipes and everything is clear
(Baker Street is blanketed in fog);
Country squires have nothing more to fear
(troubled by the conduct of a dog).

Kidnap, scandal, murder on a train –
smoke three pipes and everything is clear:
though Scotland Yard has lost the plot again
country squires have nothing more to fear.

A case in which some nasty secrets lurk –
kidnap, scandal, murder on a train?
Rolling up his sleeves he sets to work
though Scotland Yard has lost the plot again.

Watson's stories casually report
a case in which some nasty secrets lurk.
Sherlock's cocaine habit needs support:
rolling up his sleeves he sets to work.

A pattern can repeat until it palls.
Watson's stories casually report
clients crowding Mrs Hudson's halls
(Sherlock's cocaine habit needs support).

A character gets fame beyond his share.
Mysteries whirl round until they pall.
While faithful Watson's busy being there
hawklike Holmes is riding for a Fall.

OVER

He'd always liked late summer evenings
with dusk not far beyond the close of play,
white sightscreens holding back the sky
from turning amber. End of season aches
and fading light would not prevent him
measuring his run once more.
Habit rubbed the ball on flannel,
though its shine was almost gone,
to bid the genie of his past success
put polish on a final effort.

His contract not renewed; no offers
from another quarter: which, he thought,
pretty well described his love life.

Twenty paces. Now he turned
and stiff legs bent themselves to winding up
some pace and rhythm, upper body
still but tense until its pivot threw
his left arm high; and sideways-on,
full tilt, he let his eyes take one last sighting
then the spring beneath his spine
released the slingshot in his shoulder.
Front foot jarred into the earth; momentum
flung him into follow-through.

The perfect inswing hit the sea
exactly when his body pitched full-length
among the rocks below the cliff.

BANK HOLIDAY

Memories were once repeatable:
in theory he could at any time
retrace with her in words the river's curve
in Amsterdam or Reims.

Their last day out remains unfinished.
They hadn't started work on polishing
the favoured parts and making little myths
of what the boatman said

or catching in some later catch-phrase
the banter of the batsmen on the green
waiting for the next dismissal.
Moments that her eye for detail froze

lie shiny-printed, but without her gloss,
since they scanned them, only once,
on that evening when she hurried home
from a last heart-stopping trip to town.

ECHO

This late summer afternoon
is hurrying towards an evening
at a bedside. Knowing I'll be over-nighting
in an empty house, I stop
for morning milk and bread.
The shop has ice-cream flags outside:
inside it's full of fathers

and children from the new marina.
They are buying breakfast too:
it's sausages and eggs that oil and fuel the crews
but cabin boys keep nagging them
for sweets and plastic bats.
Their seaside-shop smells get me

fancying a game of cricket
on the beach, with Dad as keen
as if it was a proper match. He played till fifty
when, to Mum's alarm,
sharp singles ran him short of breath.

He once hit three successive fours.
I saw, then half a second later
heard, each one rebound against the boundary
and lobbed a cliché underarm

that made Mum laugh. And Dad as well
when he was out. And now it's bouncing
gently back: *He's got another lease of life!*

LED BY THE NOSE

From a sidestreet garage
a strange damp tang emerges, curling
like a finger switching on a memory.
The last coal merchant operating in N1
is into plastic bags and cash 'n' carry.

But coalmen I remember
wore seal-scalp leather caps,
a single flipper hanging down behind
to shield their shoulders from the lumpy cargos
like carcasses, they hefted off the lorry
down our side way, twenty at a time
in centrally unheated 'fifties Britain.

My Mum, afraid of nothing worse
than workmen's language, wanted me indoors
hinting that the white-eyes
had all done time in prison.

And she was not the last who tried to demonise
providers of the rough and ready energy
that fuelled our winter fireside society.
Anchored firm as concrete plugs
in nineteen-eighties pit shafts,
redundant coal-hole covers punctuate
the Yorkstone pavement like full stops
hammered by an iron-handed typist
with insufficient care about the shift key.

BLEAK
For R.S.Thomas

For years the coal-black priest
tried by the dim light in his head
to reach the surface of existence
where God's big hand for ever
splits infinity
like slate, His small hand
pointing always to midnight or to noon.

For years he worked as well
at the bone hard face of Huw Puw
who would not tell the time and who cared nothing
for all the spiral wisdom
of the galaxies,
whose hands were only raised
in anger, or to cut another swede.

Can anything be won
from such unyielding ground?
No answer. He choked on dust
and coughed up blood-streaked poetry.

COLD SNAP 1963

It was the mother of all snowy years
when I was driving back to you
from that single Christmas spent apart
in all the time we were together.
The roads were not defined,
merely implied by truck-wheel tracks
printed on a spread of white,
all Hampshire amplifying moonlight
in my cinematic windscreen.

There seemed no need to steer –
the deep packed ruts
ran down to Exeter like rails.
The fine-grain juddering
from miles of tread marks inside out
forced my hands to grip the wheel
and set my wrists on edge.

The thaw revealed
you and I were also driving
in circumstantial grooves
through a temporary landscape.
It may have been my rigid riding
over small irregularities
that led to the suspension breaking
suddenly next spring.

GENERIC ENGINEERING

Half the cars I ever owned are classics
now (unless they're broken up for spares)
with individual Midlands accents
beneath the piston-slap and tappet-rattle.

When English badges lost their meaning, France
still felt authentic – until a dynasty
of Citroëns rode the tumbril too.
National panache is obsolete

as fins and chromium in global showrooms:
corporate survival favours shapes
that can't be placed; selects against
species that proclaim their origin.

Comparing auto-fauna, uniformly
bland as quasi-Esperanto names,
no longer takes a connoisseur –
choose from feels less and less like *choose between*.

ONE PREVIOUS OWNER
For Stan Tracey

My car
once belonged to a Great British Jazzman.
His name's
at the top right-hand side of my log-book.
His tunes
on old home-made cassettes haunt my tape deck.

His hands
nudge the wheel as the traffic jams round me
when I
improvise a new line around Fiveways
or try
variations on Camden Town speed bumps.

The syncopated windscreen-wipers
shuffle over frost rime
and through raindrops.
The indicator's winking skips an
intermittent offbeat
during cold snaps.
The power-steering whining at the
far end of its travel
sounds a blue note.

A leak
in the tailpipe is burbling a bass line;
the gear
box is moaning a B-flat vibrato;
and so
I must double de-clutch every key change.

When I
stroke the buttons that wind down the windows
the riff
that I play sends them rising and falling
in turn
like four frontmen each taking a chorus.

TWO OUT OF FOUR

*"Django" and "One Bass Hit" are classic recordings by the
Modern Jazz Quartet. The first (a tribute to guitarist Django
Reinhardt) is a showcase piece for Milt Jackson's vibraharp, while
the second features a solo by double-bassist Percy Heath.*

Django
Guessing he'd been sentimental,
Milt stretched the aching spectral voice
within a breath of breaking:
perhaps he knew how Django skipped
and clapped his damaged hands when his own solos
were first played back to him at HMV.

East Croydon in the middle '60s
was where and when I saw the MJQ.
My companion believed me
a sophisticate for knowing
from my LP sleeves
they'd all be wearing DJs.

It was Percy's bass that lent its heartbeat
so Django's ghost could strut on stage –
but not before Milt's hammers
shaped his aura, shimmering
like white sound surging to the everlasting
centre of a 78.

One bass hit
His likeness
in an icon
would be scarcely out of place:
that radiance of polished forehead
could be a halo taking shape.

Unsmiling
as an angel
he brought stillness – plus a pulse –
intensifying melody
as incense can enhance a prayer.

MILES

There is frost on the verges
and he is playing *Summertime*.
Each note unwinds the road a hundred yards
in the film that's showing on my windscreen.

In front of the camera
I have wanted, many times,
to be the one who changed the storyline,
and played a scene the way it wasn't written.

To accept I'm an extra
is getting easier each time
directors keep the take the star ad-libbed
and then, to match, they cut and splice the seasons.

GAS STATION
The 1940 Edward Hopper painting

Evening on a road you might remember;
last chance for fuel before the dusky mountains.
You fill up, tell the man how far you've come
then rear-view glimpse him start to close the place
as if he'd kept it open just for you
to take and place him in that rosary
whose beads are wayside accidents and graces
strung on a time-lapse image of your tail-lights.

A CAPITAL CHRISTMAS

Trim the tree
Award a star for good behaviour
then find the fairy who might turn us
into how we'd like to see ourselves
by the reassuring glow
of coloured lights colluding with the dark.
Hang the holly to adorn
the door so sprigs of prickles symbolize
our greetings. Set the mistletoe
to lure someone to kiss and make us royal,
removing spells we're crouching under.
Meanwhile rummage in the cupboard
for that missing box of decorations.
Count the cards again. Ignore
the nagging feeling something's been forgotten.

Deck the malls
Was the sponsored dove in Regent Street
the freeze-dried Holy Spirit? Were the angels
and the shepherds praising Pure New Wool?
Did cattle round a crib by Matroncare
sport logos with good news of British beef?

The kings have not arrived, but Magi Motels
have their rooms reserved. With Bright Star Travel
they will be in time for farewell drinks
with Simeon (who leaves with peace of mind
accorded by his Faith Fund AVCs).

But then what? An Egyptian getaway
is fine but what's the point of all that business
with the children? Violence has its place,
of course; but certain people haven't learned
when to leave good stories well alone.

CALL CENTRE

Welcome to the Supplication Hotline;
and thankyou that you chose to call
Judaeo-Christian Heaven with your problem.

To help us deal effectively with your requests,
if you own a touch-tone rosary
please go directly to the Joyful Mysteries ...

Thankyou. Now if you're looking for
success in business or exams
press 1 and then prioritise your goals.

If you'd like luck in love or lottery
press 2; but note that in these areas
terms and conditions may apply.

For health concerns press 3; and please
be ready with the name and list of symptoms.
If however someone has already died
press 4 to hear a word of consolation.

Please note that, following a user survey,
since the start of this millennium
confession and repentance options
have been withdrawn till further notice.

To assist continuing improvement
of our service you may instead press 5
and tell our After-Benediction Section
if our response to your request falls short
of mission statement guarantees.

If you possess an older hand- or mind-set
and would prefer to talk directly
to our representative
please hold the line:
but we are obliged by law to warn you
such conversations may be monitored.

MINE HOST

You get all sorts turning up in here –
everyone gets tired and thirsty on the road;
lots of foreigners of course
but mostly I don't take much notice of them.

Still, this stranger that I'm telling you about –
him you couldn't help but notice.
Well it wasn't really him, it was
the other one. Half-dead he was and bleeding.

I didn't want to know. It looked like trouble.
But the stranger said he'd take responsibility.
So I put them in a corner while he fussed around
like the victim's brother – which he surely wasn't!

I went to bed myself and left them to it
and in the morning things looked slightly better –
until I found the foreigner was leaving
and wanted me to join his caring game.

At least he'd sense to make it worth my while:
paid up front for five days room and board
and agreed to cover all the extras.
(In my place you just can't be too careful).

I suppose you're working out what's coming next:
feed the invalid on bread and water,
turn him out as soon as he can walk
and then start making up the bill.

All right, between ourselves, it did go through my mind
while the foreigner and I were talking terms.
In my place others would have thought the same.
(Why not? No-one ever does us favours).

But pretty soon I knew it wouldn't happen.
The stranger seemed so sure I'd treat them right.
Yes that's the point: it was all a touch too easy.
(Somewhere, sometimes you've got to draw the line).

There's gossip says I finished out-of-pocket;
but you know how these rumours get about.
Anyone can talk. The simple truth is this:
being soft won't keep a man in business.

ALDEBURGH
For Roy Blackman

Keep going till the easterly extreme.
Miss out the Maltings. In the final mile
ignore the bungalows and B&B's
for urban transients; pass by the church
and, almost last of all, the lifeboat station
till you find yourself on shelving shingle.

To the north, beyond the Sizewell hum,
the coastline's edging backward. Slabs of wheatfield
slump and crumble on that beach where rows
of hopeful one-more-plantings feed the waves.
But here you drop down to the sea obliquely,
pebbles pulling at your heels like puppies.

Hauled-in fishing boats give names and numbers;
skippers' netted windows look beyond
your shoulder at the shallow-breathing ocean.
Beneath its oily sulkiness how many
Dorniers and Wellingtons went down
from nineteen-thirty-nine to the horizon?

Sailboat colours splash isosceles
on grey November canvas. Here come poets
prowling front and back streets, chattering
like children on an outing, each one clutching
dinner money.
                         They're all strangers here:
there's little point in asking them the way.

A MATTER OF APPEARANCES
For Michael Standen

Only in (or is it from?) this dream
you've not yet departed.
But you know you will be going;
so with gruff defiance
you are summarising your intentions
straight to camera
ignoring what's outside your eye line
while the rest of us
stand close in mutual consolation.

Now you're saying something else
about a famous poet
whose name immediately escapes me –
he left a hidden message
encouraging all proto-socialists
and contrived a puzzle
(with scattered clues for its solution)
to enable its discovery
and subsequent post-mortem publication.

I wonder if this tale is any truer
than your stated tastes
in boating: silent use of a canoe
for sliding in alongside
film sets on location seeking close-ups
of manufactured action
from an unintended angle.
None of the producers
could persuade you you were trespassing.

MUM'S BRIDGE

Coming back from cakes and tea in Buckingham
we glimpsed it on our left, by-passed by recent tarmac,
spared for safety's sake from taking juggernauts.
We stopped and walked it. Oddly, she went out in front
and had to turn her head to smile on hearing me
misnaming, more or less routinely, some wild flower.
She crossed the narrow stream ahead of all of us,
having had a good day, not quite over.

ABSENT WITHOUT LEAVING

I wasn't there to take the call
and only heard third-hand the news
she didn't want me to expect.

She'd lived so long within herself
to slip from sight, cause no distress,
become a voice inside the phone.
The message meant these obstacles
were obsolete and it was time
to face the truth, that here and now
I'd ever and forever missed
the point of her departure.

We both denied ourselves goodbyes
small-talking on an empty platform
as if the train could never come.

CONTINUITY

He knew that they'd be frightened of his feelings.
He could have worked it out
while they were scuttling up the motorway;
or in that extra time he had for thinking
as they failed to take the shortest route
to him across the city:
first the fruitless detour to the hospital
where he'd already left the empty-bedside;
then the corner shop
to pick up milk and thick-sliced Mother's Pride
they thought he might be short of.

He saw the car crawl up the hill and stop;
watched them climbing out
and fumbling with the gate; then almost ran
to open up the front door for them
and admit their hesitation.
It's me, I'm still the same, he reassured them.

SURFACE REACTION

The last thing that he saw her touch
was a cut-glass cruet.
Afterwards he searched its surface angles
for a fingerprint
to prove there was some corner
where identity persisted,
in loops indisputably her own.

Could he crystallize the essence
in this touch of tissue?
Or with scientific tricks succeed
in drawing out its spirals
like a spring to find
the spirit of her double helix
and being less hellishly alone?

A dozen prisms
caught his speculation
and split it to its simplest colours,
whose names he would formerly have known.

SEVENTY-TWO

It's not the way your mother made.
He meant the Yorkshire pudding
and the light but crusty comment
rose perfectly to complement
his well-pressed gabardine and tie.

It pleased him, on his birthday,
to be distinguished from the shirtsleeved
open-necked and untucked
uniformity of Sunday pubs
favoured by his son-in-law.

His daughter, turning forty,
was growing more and more familiar
and worrying his memory;
he thoughtfully allowed himself
to take that second glass of beer
her mother would have frowned at.

THIN END

My grandmother was ruthlessly right-handed.
The left was merely a restraint she used
for pinning springy loaves beneath the bread-knife
as she sawed off raft-like sandwiches
for her husband's tea break. Bottom halves,
he told me once, would always come up thicker.

Years were sliced away: they closed the docks
so grandad had no place to take his snap-tin.
Meanwhile her oblique repeated pressure
was wearing down the breadboard like a wedge
and editing its maker's homely motto
to the promise-free injunction that she WASTE NOT.

A DREAM OF EMPIRE

Great Uncle went abroad to find a future
planting tea. Or, more precisely,
clerking in an office to ensure
that quantities of tea were shipped.
Great Aunt stayed behind, expecting
she might see him once a year
until he'd laid a place for her
and forwarded the invitation.

The dutiful were honoured like the dead
when they ventured far beyond
the iron reach of railways
to spread the British way of life
thinly on a slice of India.
Those not home for Christmas
had their absence toasted soberly;
and The Company sent large and tasteless cards
to their children on each birthday.

SOMEONE HAD TO

*Samuel Plimsoll MP, "the seaman's friend", campaigned for safe
loading limits for ships*

Being on the ship that didn't sink –
the one in five survivor – made him
somebody who had to cry
enough of coffin ships that wallowed
out to sea with overloads of risk,
police-escorted to deep water –
no escape for crews across the side that law and order took.

He manned his campaign platforms with their widows.
Veiled and silent walls of sadness
loomed behind him, night by night
relentlessly, like long black waves
to add momentum to his rhetoric
for overcoming one by one
the flagships of the owners' lines of unseaworthy arguments.

How often there is something going on
it's clear someone should try to stop:
how seldom someone does – and gets
small thanks until they're good and dead.

His Bill, thrown overboard by Parliament,
was salvaged as one small, bedraggled
clause on painting loading levels –
at the company's discretion.
Freeboard being fixed might harm free trade
so anywhere would do below
the deckrail or the funnel: coasters could still ride as low as barges.

He worked himself to death to get the lines
set properly by seas and seasons.
And near-drowned men did not forget:
mourners stripped off Sunday best
then let the sweating, black-plumed horses go
and took their place to pull his hearse
like galley slaves who'd volunteered for this one coffin's
homeward run.

When someone's good and dead, the things they changed
are how things are: the way things were
is what they took on board until
they were submerged way past their safety line.

NATIONAL SERVICEMAN

Designed between a pair of wars
then built by many hands in many lands
one pattern was stamped out across an Empire:
two floors of standard rooms to form
three-dimensioned Union Jacks
foursquare among the flagstones.

It might have brought security
(peace of mind if not the other sort)
to know his place whatever his location;
but he was haunted by the thought
of one day going through a door,
say in Aldershot tomorrow,
and finding nineteen thirty-eight in Singapore.

HOME FRONT

Oh good, you've got some leave, she said.
She called it out across the day-room
re-inventing National Service:
his absences at Catterick
until demob and marriage in the fifties.

He was used to gathering
her memories like faded ribbons
trailing from a broken maypole:
a gentleman or officer
should take her arm and join her in the dance.

Over strong sweet tea and talk
of ration books, what he remembered,
clear and sudden as a fragrance,
was walking homeward in short trousers
on a wartime Wiltshire autumn evening.

On the undulating road
down to the village green a bike
came ticking through the dusk, and turning
he'd plainly recognized his father.
But hindsight said he must have been at Arnhem.

BATTLE TRAINING

I'm oddly glad my father went to France in 'forty-four,
saw action and could tell me what he'd seen – or some of it.
All I can claim is that I slept while bombs dropped on the docks
and must have heard a doodlebug splutter out its threat.

But who'd been there to let him know about the other side?
His oldest brother might have talked about the Somme campaign
if he'd not disappeared into the mud of no man's land
with nothing left behind except his absence to explain.

Dad found an unspent cartridge once (perhaps a point two-two)
when he was six or seven playing over by the pier
and bigger boys had gone to join the game to end all games.
He took it home to show a friend, a budding engineer,

who clamped it in a vice and struck it sharply with a spike.
The bullet ricocheted around the shed from roof to wall
but missed his baffled head: and though it bounced at him again,
embattled outside Caen, he wouldn't have a closer call.

SWORD BEACH

It's here our forebears clambered from the sea
and survival on more hostile ground began –
a struggle to determine what would be
the changing shape of European Man –
    selected as the fittest time and place
    to cut the crap about a master race.

Casinos crashed ahead of the advance
(the house had never lost so much before);
but still a thousand private games of chance
with rising stakes were played along the shore.
    And tickets too were everywhere on sale
    for state-run raffles on a massive scale.

The set was thin with nothing made to last:
by rust or bullets destined to be holed.
Not much was spent on costumes, for the cast
were mostly extras if the truth be told.
    Well out of shot they mounted an attack
    dressed up to kill in facemask and a mac.

The beach was crowded for the time of year
when visitors turned up from out of town.
Above the shoreline not an inch was clear:
they fought to get a space for lying down.
    Some sleepers in the sandhills never learned
    to look for shade and they were badly burned.

The papers said that casualties were light.
Who weighed them as they lifted off a limb?
Or did a count of wounds improve the sight
of eyes that by the evening had gone dim?
    Pronouncements on the loss we can afford
    should end with *next of kin have been ignored.*

LEAVING THE VETERANS' HOME

Beyond the patio
(where ex-master-sergeant Wall would snarl
and scrape up pigeon dirt)
behind the picture window
of the day-room he stood waving,
smiling through Canadian double glazing
which kept excluding more and more
of what was once familiar.

He stayed there till I couldn't see him
as if he knew I wouldn't see him any more
before a coma closed the curtain
six months afterwards
while we were seven hours apart.

Our daytimes didn't even match
and England was, for him, a hazy prelude
to a war in which his skills at hunting
white-tailed deer and blue-winged teal
were commandeered for ambushes and sniping.

Now on this still-dark London morning
as I set down the telephone
I'm the one who's left inside
while he's outdoors again
and re-inventing an old pleasure:
blending into unknown landscape
and enjoying getting closer
to a quarry that he's yet to see.

The odd thing is
that when I pull aside the drapes
he'll still be waving to me.

ALBERT

Na' then,
he would say,
to tell us he expected our attention;
and the flat South Yorkshire vowels
were stacked up ready for a change of subject.

Na' then, lad,
he'd greet me every visit
to let me know I had the floor
to tell him how I'd been and how I'd come –
by which route around the roadworks
slowing down his city's heart.
His pride was still his skill to pick
the best way over seven hills from A to B.

Na' then
began each reminiscence for the children,
Grandad unabashed by repetition:
This partickler tale I'm goin' to tell
you've heard before
but anyhow I'll tell it you again
to let you know how things have changed
since I were your age.

Now he's gone
the further change has been
not just a trip from A to B:
Na', more like from A ter bloody Z.

LUMB BANK
The writers' retreat in Yorkshire

Earth waits behind the house,
camouflaged in brown or green by seasons,
pressing, patient, on the sag-bricked wall
with courses crushed to slow-flow plasticene.
Stones do better, keeping station
to sustain a man-shaped curve
toward the road. The lintel's split
above a gate that leads to nowhere;
weeds have wriggled through its frame.

Some would-be writers mock successful tradesmen
who ventured to erect high places
over valleys where their wealth was built.
Which seems unfair now that I'm borrowing
their barriers for holding back
the tides of entropy and gravity.
Here in this head-held elbow-room
where they made space for libraries and gardens
I take uneasy profits from their enterprise.

RIEVAULX ABBEY

*In the 21st century the abbey finds itself beneath airspace used by
the RAF for pilot training*

How would the abbots understand
these trainee aerobats
who carve erratic patterns overhead?
As flocks of growling omen-birds?
Or as yet more novices
grappling with the mastery of heaven?

Those who piloted these arches,
making loops and spirals
out of stone, not fading vapour trails,
meant to set apart a space
that demonstrates devotion
to the graceful mysteries of heaven.

But, near the ground, a down-gust sometimes
strips your lift away
so even angel wings must stall and tumble;
survival's then a matter of
pragmatic airmanship
more than pure ideas of flight dynamics.

THE BRITISH AIRCRAFT INDUSTRY, CIRCA 1966

Donald's involved in a government contract
about slender deltas and laminar flow;
he's busy with transforms and multiple integrals –
equations and formulae row upon row.

Gerald is dozing and dreaming of Wimbledon
(his sister gets tickets because of her work);
he's meant to be checking some data with Ronald
who spots a mistake, wakes him up with a jerk.

And outside the bombers are lined up and ready
to roll down the runway, rotate into flight;
but these are mere prototypes, empty of armament
and no one will raid anybody tonight.

Oswald's a draughtsman with red hair and glasses
a check shirt and beard and he's gone a bit soft
on the charms and the shape of the blonde busty tracer
who lays out the spars and the ribs in the loft.

And outside the bombers are lined up awaiting
conversion to tankers – or else to be scrapped
or crammed full of cameras for photo-reconnaissance
ensuring all Russia is thoroughly mapped.

Recently made up to manager, Reginald
wears a black homburg, but you'd never guess
this big honey-bear man in crumpled blue trousers
is head of the office that takes care of stress.

And outside the bombers are lined up and rusting.
These small British cousins of B-52s
relied on their pilots: now governments favour
anonymous bombing – cruise missiles, not crews.

FLYING UNDER BRIDGES

Huddled in the Avro with her nose
turned up against the horizontal snow
Wop opened up the throttle and she rose
but only just: the bridge was higher than she'd go.

In a flash of saved-up *déjà vu*
his slipstream raked the North Saskatchewan
as, fuelled by pure adrenaline, he flew
between High Level legs, beneath that black lace span

carrying some memory or rumour
of Kathy Stinson's thighs the way that once
Lou Fosseneuve, for a bishop he must humour,
ran Athabasca rapids with a bunch of nuns.

Now at thirty-two degrees below
it was Peace River bridge above his head
and serum barely warm beside his toes
for Doctor Hammon waiting with his dogs and sled

in Fort Vermilion where they had to prise
poor frozen Wop and Vic out of their places
while radio sent praises to the skies
about Alberta's rediscovered pair of aces.

While they headed home their hearts still fluttered
wondering how long a motor runs
on dirty fuel: the way it coughed and stuttered
was like the final spit of von Richthofen's guns.

Wilfred "Wop" May was a WW1 fighter pilot from Alberta who took part in the
dog-fight in which the Red Baron, Manfred von Richthofen, was killed. Among his
peace-time exploits was a flight under Edmonton's High Level Bridge in 1919.
Wop had to repeat this trick at Peace River in 1926 when, with Vic Horner, he was
flying in medical supplies to deal with an outbreak of diphtheria.

Katherine Stinson was an American stunt pilot who performed at Edmonton
1916-1918. Her flying clothes – tight jodhpurs – aroused as much comment as
her aerobatics.

Louis "Sure shot" Fosseneuve in 1867 transported five Grey Nuns along the then
dangerously low Athabasca River at the request of Bishop Faraud.

43

AT THE PONT DU GARD
Len Hutton, batsman

Leg and middle please, I might have said
as we approached the massive wickets
of the Pont du Gard
where, among the sellers of soft soaps,
a day-old English tabloid told me
a cricketer had died.

All the papers wanted to recall
was how he'd won the Ashes back
in Coronation Year;
but study of an ancient *Wisden* told me
how, in 'thirty-eight, he drove
Australian bowlers like a gang of slaves
and built a three-decked aqueduct of runs
to span dry seasons
with a flow of English self-respect.

ELECTRIC STRADIVARIUS
Leo Fender, guitar maker

In English classroom English, "fender"
used to mean a fireguard which
figured in crime fiction as
a novel instrument of death.
(*I didn't 'ardly touch 'im, guv,*
'e fell and 'it 'is 'ead.)

A facelift in the fifties as
the transatlantic synonym
for mudguard or for bumper bar
did not deflect the destiny
of "fender": it was meant to be
identified with Leo.

He mass-produced Excaliburs
for brandishing by heroes who
prevailed against those dragons Taste
and Moderation, cutting down
the creepers choking closed the doors
of dungeon Well-Behaved.

He built it too for smaller mortals,
miming riffs in private moments,
imitating power chords
to howl above the workday drone –
for spirit swells and pride uncurls
when Stratocaster speaks.

BARBERSHOP FANTASY

The barber's aging hi-fi
jerks, then drags Ravel's *Bolero*
like a comb through matted curls.
Them cheap tapes stretch, he tells me, adding
People out of proper orchestras
live around here now: back in the fifties
all there was was seamen's digs and clip-joints.

That shiver isn't from the razor
teasing small hairs from my neck.
It's the breeze as Maltese matelots
ghost-dance their molls through one more tango.
Sleek and sequined, they brush gently
past a boy who needs a padded board
to occupy this grown-up chair.

APPRECIATING T.S. ELIOT

Eighteen is a foolish age, mingling
caution with bravado. Having risked
the slim blue Faber volume I confined
my first attentions to the contents page.

And his titles were so good!
What must the poetry itself be like?
How in tune with moody adolescence
to write of wastelands and of hollow men!

How reassuring Prufrock's name
to one acquainted with old Henry Crun
and Major Bloodnok. Here was a kindred spirit,
a pioneer who had foreseen the Goons.

On getting past the index of first lines
my understanding failed; but he succeeded
in getting past my misconceptions,
coolly planting words that put down roots

and phrases whose uneasy fragrance lingered
for another twenty years, awaiting
more mature approval. I began
among the different voices to discern

the prophet who was speaking out
of rocky shadows cast by truth
across the sunny places where we lie
enjoying too much unreality.

A CHAT WITH DYLAN THOMAS

Words rolled from him like syrup off a knife,
or as water drops
released with perfect surface tension
from frozen house-tops fondled by a winter sun.

A chuckle like dark chocolate runs through
each story offered as we stroll
the snow-packed Mumbles, peeping in
past parlour drapes. He wants me to appreciate

the way hot-ladled flavours crystallise
to tasty melting sweets; but laughs
to see me try to label them
and, with my mouth full, think I'll get the recipe.

CK IN ChCh*

James called him Karl.
The rest of us laCKed
the nerve to call him
anything. He had the knaCK
of making us glad
simply to listen.

We wanted to tuCK
into a supper but
the Twisted Hop
was paCKed so we popped
next door to Red JaCK's.

James chose the mussels.
He piCKed something else -
whatever it was
the girl came straight baCK
and said it was off.
So he had duCK inSTEAD.

*ChCh is the local abbreviation for Christchurch, New Zealand

POLYMATH
i.m. JJM

I wished that I could sing like him –
full-throat, full-throttle
hand-flat rhythm on the table-top.
He drove an Irish rebel ballad
through double thicknesses
of smoke and chatter in a Tuscan bar
and the haze of noise and fumes
our ears and sinuses were filled with
since the Fiat Cinquecento's engine
at our backs had clattered
like an avalanche of spoons
between the antipasto and the grappa.

The next day found him
in a mood to speculate
about, for instance, Socrates' initials.
Among the vines that striped a hill
below the birthplace of a Pope
he readily acknowledged
Render unto Caesar was
a damn good answer to a tricky question.
Was it at the concrete works we toured
(the Holy Father's home was closed)
that he began the not-so-abstract problem
what belongs to God?

FINISHING TOUCH
A tour guide's story about Alvar Aalto

On that Sunday
the architect was there to watch
the congregation's first immersion in his pool
of colours. He'd selected richest pigments
for the frescoes and the glass:
they had chosen mostly sober clothing

and dropped in place
before the altar stiffly as
piano hammers practising familiar scales.
Then a single umber overcoat
among the greys and herringbones
fell exactly where his hope was pointing

straight below
the vertex of the birchwood crucifix.
Then he could tell himself he heard a flourish fading
down the long connecting corridor
another master builder used
to slip in unannounced and place the keystone.

GOING GENTLY
For Gertrude Buckman

Hearing's usually the last to go,
the nurse confided –
and she would be herself the last to stay
with comfortable words for you.

Love would have liked to have a chance
to offer you a final lullaby
that would not falter even though
the steadier the song
the sooner you'd be lost to utter sleep .
But you'd have felt it put you under
obligation if, to ease your pain,
someone went to any trouble.
You liked care on level terms.

But you could still have had a chance
of finding love un-disappointing
for all its past and clumsy blunders;
of understanding how surrender puts
to bed that sense of obligation.
It would have mattered even less
than yesterday if you'd accepted gifts
as simple as a bottle of good wine
or complex as an overwhelming grace.

BROKEN RHYTHM

The first mistakes occurred a few days later.
A wrongly primed alarm
meant the buzzer, not the radio,
sliced across my oversleep,
coarse-grinding dreams made extra dark
by roasting in my skull too long.

Habit, half-awake, poured two strong coffees.
Neither one was drunk
of course: I had to leave without the surge
of virtue from embracing black
and bitter instant substitutes
for purposeful deliberation.

When I came back, the bedside clock was flashing
a red and stupid time.
Another local power cut had left it
stunned, to try and catch the sun
again by futile beating
like a butterfly against a window.

All the poor thing needed was somebody
else to be at home
when I was out to set it right and steady
down its frantic fluttering.
It would have been as easy as
it was to say defibrillation.

ROLE MODELS, 1994
i.m. LBB

I remember you and Ayrton Senna
hurtling through the tunnel under Monte Carlo
with sufficient downforce to stick us to the roof
then bursting out with laughter into sunshine.

That striving always for some extra speed
and latest braking into every corner –
even chasing pole in Waitrose car park –
ended in a sudden spinning out
beyond a bend not reckoned with.

I remember you and Denis Potter
hurting, as you tried to overcome discomfort
with relentless reading, late-night tapes
to stop sensation speaking all too frankly.

All you had to hide behind was skin
far from being thick as many thought.
They missed the optimism in bad news
faced squarely, and they never peddled you
a crock of immortality.

GRAVEYARD SHIFT

Perhaps it's easier to raise the dead
than rouse the living.
The former are supposed to turn their toes up:
the latter dig them in
against what might not let them rot in peace.

Dead men, so we hear, do not tell tales.
But when embarrassed
the quick are seldom slow at making stories
for covering themselves,
exhuming other people's skeletons.

LAZARUS WITHIN

Which among us will be first
to roll it away?

Experience warns us ugly things
squirm out like smells
from under stones
when we disturb them.
The same applies to sealed tombs
where flesh has been decaying
for as many days as we remember.
Once we let in light and air
we have to stomach what comes out
and most of us will want a pause for breath
before we try to cope with so much stink.

Anyone can talk of resurrection but
doubt is somewhat heavier than rock.
Move that mountain, then the rest is easy.

JOSEPH OF ARIMATHEA

How to put this so you'll understand?
Death did not diminish him –
did not disturb one truth he planted
nor distort the hopes he offered.
It was simply, having heard enough,
the world had gone back to its work –
too good for them, we might have said
if he hadn't warned us not to.

Yet it seemed the only things to do
were fetch the proper oils and shroud
and organise a fitting burial.
                    *
But, thank God, it wasn't up to us
to keep it going, somehow
holding on to clues he left;
to celebrate his life
by maintaining him a grave;
to speak enough of him for others
and ourselves to be persuaded
truth alone rebuilds a world.

He accepted, briefly, what we'd done
then broke our last best effort like a shell
whose emptiness was now its whole importance.

THOMAS

I'd not collude with anyone's delusions.
I always called a spade its proper name
and could grasp its purpose well enough
when something needed burying.
Wasn't I the first who pointed out
how we could die with him? And in broad daylight
that was, well ahead of Simon acting
all dramatic at the dinner table.

He's dead, I said, so don't you let him down
by making myths of what you want to hope
about a man who always told the truths
he saw, however hard they were.

Someone had to dig them out. I thought
that I could get the very leverage
I'd need by resting on a point of substance
and blunt impossibility.
But when I set my hand to it then something
yielded to my touch and all the firmness
of my former grip was lost: and, yes,
I do remember how it felt.

Versions of some poems in this collection appeared first in the following magazines: *Acumen, Brittle Star, The Coffee House, Critical Survey, Dreamcatcher, Envoi, The Frogmore Papers, The Interpreter's House, Obsessed with Pipework, Other Poetry, Poetry Monthly, Quattrocento, River King Poetry Supplement, The Rue Bella, Seam, Smiths Knoll, Spokes, Staple* and *Weyfarers.* Some were also included in the anthologies *In the Company of Poets* (Hearing Eye, 2003), *Take Five* (Shoestring, 2003), *Paging Doctor Jazz* (Shoestring, 2004) and *Speaking English* (Five Leaves, 2007). My sincere thanks are due to the editors of all these publications – and especially to John Lucas of Shoestring Press – for all the hard work that they devote to connecting new poetry with an audience.

I must also express my gratitude to all members, past and present, of the Cross Street poetry workshop for numerous evenings of mutual encouragement and constructive criticism. Most of all my love and thanks go to Nancy Mattson, but for whom many of these poems would never have been written.